At Home in the
TIDE POOL

Alexandra Wright • Marshall Peck III

For my mother, my teachers, and the leaders
of the Environmental Science Program
— AW

For Beth Mira Aimée Benjamin Tracy
Matt Huguette Ann Chris MHP Jr.
— MHP III

⚓ Charlesbridge

Along the rocky seashore there are many things to see. At low tide, water makes pools in the spaces between the rocks. These tide pools trap many creatures who cannot swim away until the next high tide. The tide pools are also home to many creatures that live all their lives in this little world.

lichen on rocks

Irish moss

green algae
(seaweed)

channeled wrack

The tide pool is a good home for these periwinkles. They are grazing on seaweed just like cows grazing on grass. Each periwinkle moves slowly on its one foot, scraping up food with its coiled tongue. If you knock a periwinkle off, it will pull back into its shell and close a little trap door called an operculum.

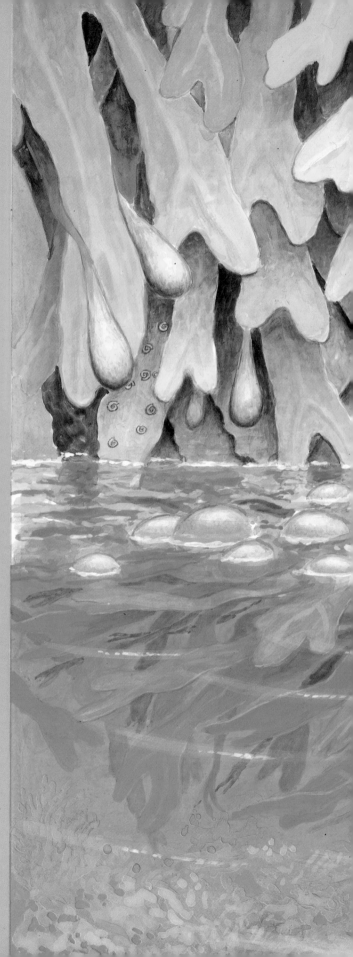

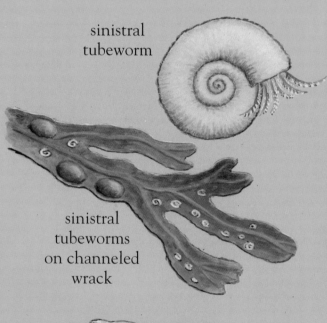

sinistral
tubeworm

sinistral
tubeworms
on channeled
wrack

periwinkle with
operculum closed

One periwinkle is moving toward something that looks like a flower, but it is an animal called a sea anemone. The parts that look like petals are its arms, or tentacles. The anemone is not waving its tentacles to say hello. It is trying to catch food. The tentacles have stinging cells, but don't worry, the sting is too weak to harm you.

When the anemone feels something it can't eat, like a person's finger, it pulls in its tentacles and shrinks down to a small blob.

bushy backed sea slug

scarlett sea cucumber

vase tunicate

Here's a cute little shrimp. It is carrying its babies in a pouch on its belly like a kangaroo! The anemones try to catch the shrimp for lunch, but it paddles away out of reach. Anemones and other tide pool animals that are stuck in one place have to spend a lot of time waiting for food to float by.

Some creatures in the tide pool can swim around to find food. The only ones that can eat the stinging tentacles of an anemone are the sea slugs. Here comes a hungry sea slug now!

twelve-scaled worm

salmon gilled
sea slug

frilled
anemone

This periwinkle is hungry, too. It has come a long way, inching along the rocks on its one rubbery foot. These rocks are covered by lumpy bread crumb sponge. A sponge is a simple animal that has no stomach or brain. It filters food out of the water through thousands of small sponge holes.

Now the periwinkle will stop to visit with its cousins, the cone-shaped limpets, the eight-plated chitons, and the piggy-backed slipper shells.

limpet

slipper shells

chiton

bread crumb sponge

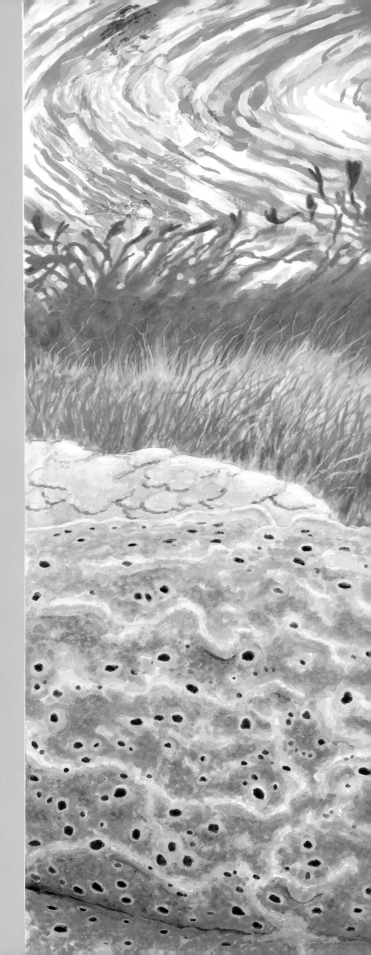

Another periwinkle wanders into a bed of Irish moss just as three crabs surprise each other. Each one scoots off sideways to find a new place to hide.

One green crab has cracked open its shell because it has grown too big for it. A rock crab is stepping right out of its old shell. Until these crabs grow new, bigger shells, they have no way to protect themselves.

The rock crab is going to do something really amazing. While it is growing a new shell, it will regrow its missing leg and claw!

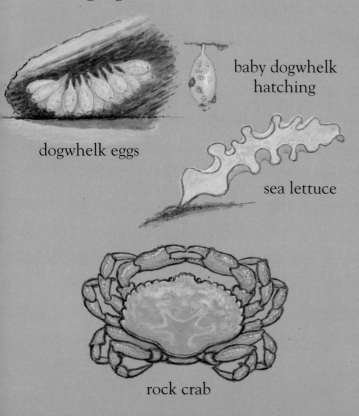

baby dogwhelk hatching

dogwhelk eggs

sea lettuce

rock crab

Some periwinkles seem to be moving much faster than others. They are not periwinkles at all! These are hermit crabs that live in empty periwinkle shells.

One of these hermits is looking for a bigger home. It knocks politely on a whelk shell to see if it is empty. The ferocious whelk is still alive and using its shell so the hermit crab scuttles away.

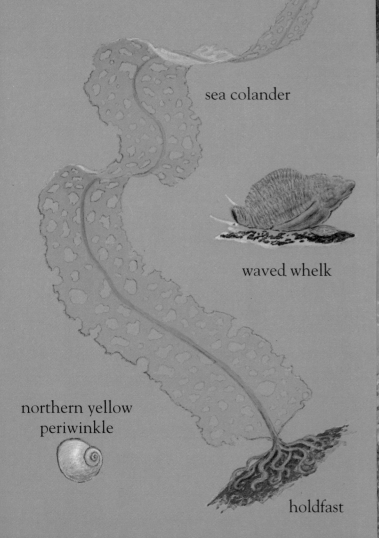

sea colander

waved whelk

northern yellow periwinkle

holdfast

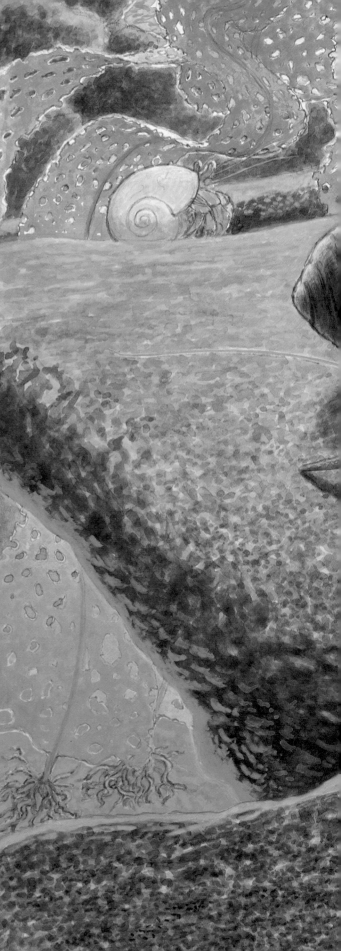

All of a sudden, the incoming tide brings in a wave that changes this quiet place into a noisy one. Periwinkles stop grazing and hold on tight. A hungry starfish uses its tiny tube feet to keep its place. It is close to its favorite food — mussels.

The mussels are stuck to the rocks with tough threads. They can move by spinning new threads and cutting the old ones, but this is too slow to escape from the hungry starfish.

kelp

bysis holding
mussel threads

kelp
holdfast

stalked tunicate

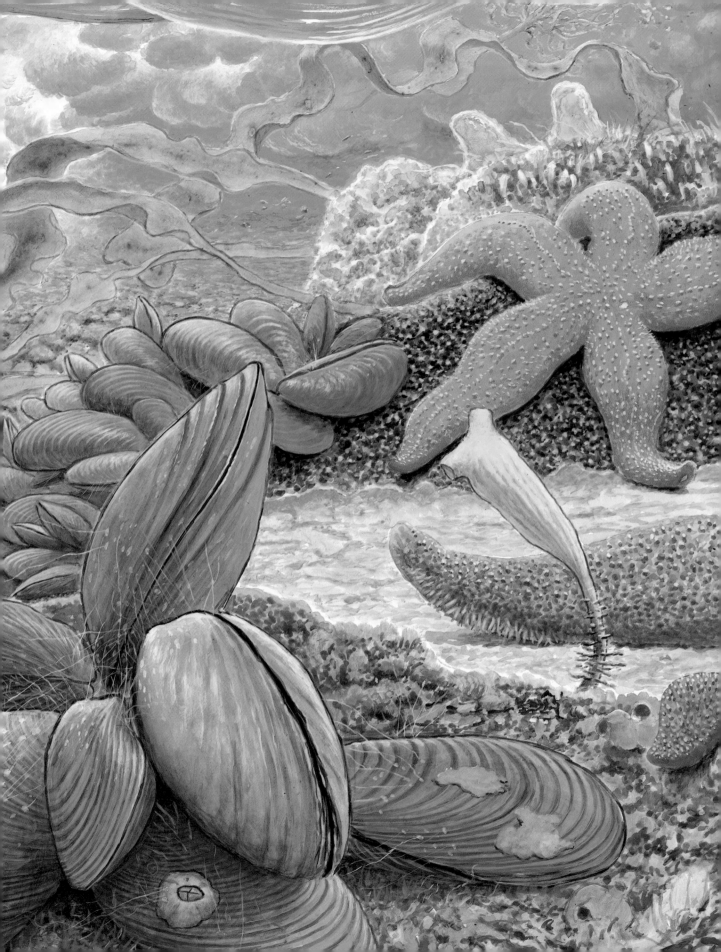

When the mussels feel the starfish coming, they clamp their shells shut. The starfish wraps itself around a mussel and uses its rows of suckers to pry apart the two halves of the mussel shell. The starfish will push its own stomach out through its mouth and into the mussel. After it eats the mussel, the starfish pulls its stomach back where it belongs!

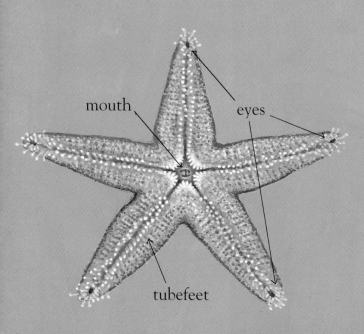

mouth

eyes

tubefeet

starfish

The starfish has moved too close to the stinging tentacles of an anemone. The anemone grabs a starfish leg, pulls it off, and eats it! The starfish scrambles away on its other four legs. It will grow a new leg to replace the missing one.

The crashing waves move a boulder that breaks off another one of the starfish's legs. The leg washes into the bottom of the tide pool where, believe it or not, it will grow into a whole new starfish!

skate egg case

purple algae

green sea urchin

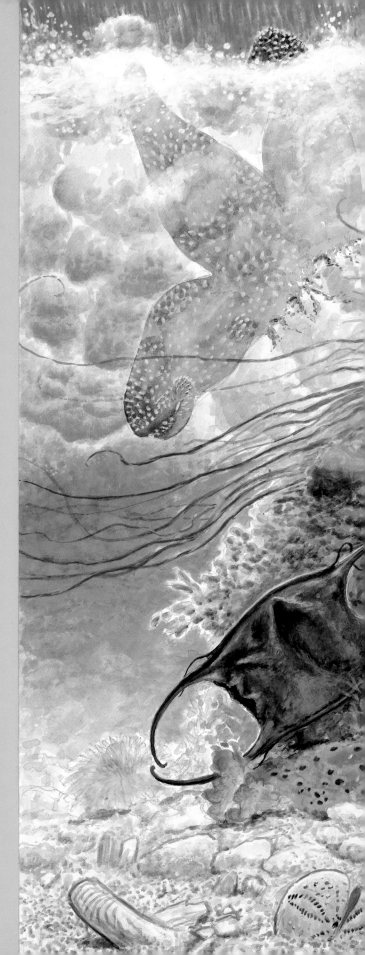

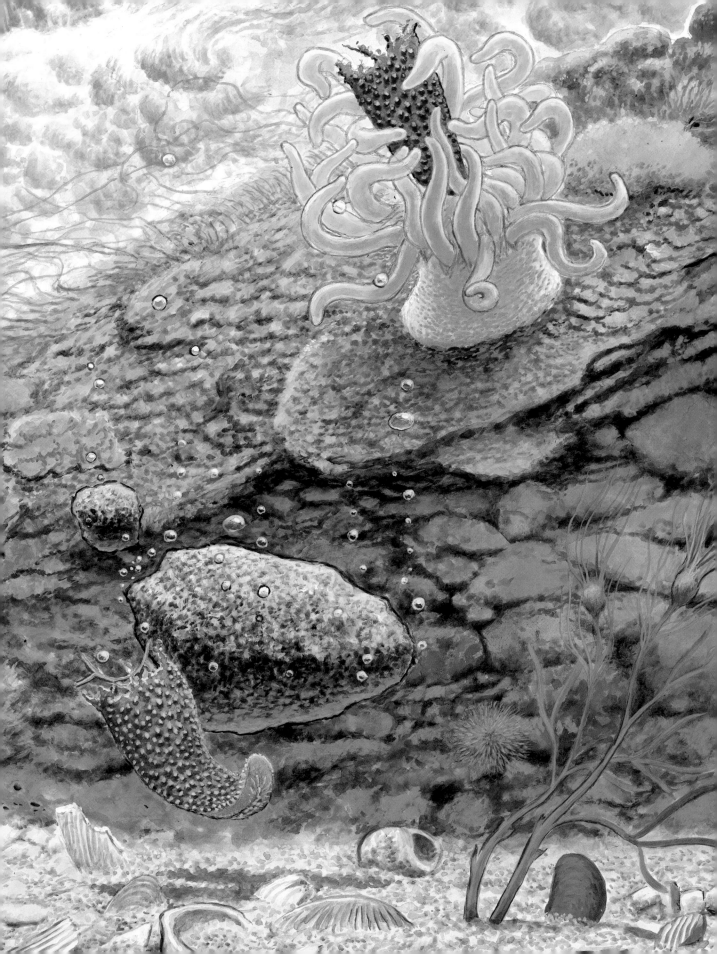

The three-legged starfish takes cover in a bed of rockweed. Below, a pile of empty mussel shells with neat round holes is a sign that dogwinkles have been here.

Most relatives of periwinkles are planteaters, but not the dogwinkle. It eats mussels, barnacles, and clams. It grinds a perfectly round hole right through their shells. Then it sucks out the animal inside.

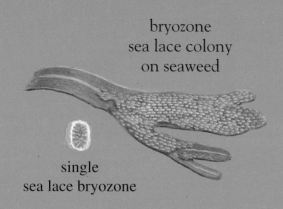

bryozone
sea lace colony
on seaweed

single
sea lace bryozone

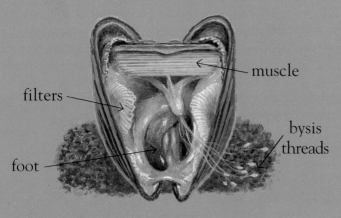

muscle

filters

bysis
threads

foot

inside of a mussel

A young octopus swims in with a big wave. It lives in a narrow hole in the outer rocks. Like a magician it changes color quickly and blends in with the colors of the tide pool. Swimming is very different for an octopus because its legs grow out of one side of its head and its body grows out of the other side! This octopus is so hungry that it left its dark home in the daytime. The crab that it grabs to eat does not have a chance of escaping.

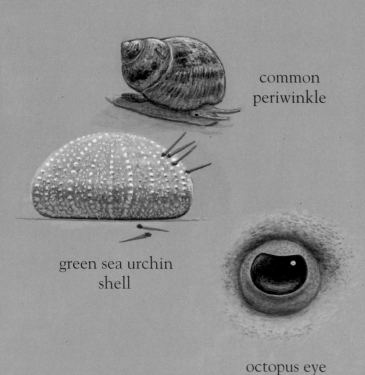

common periwinkle

green sea urchin shell

octopus eye

It is high tide now. You can see the mussels opening up to feed. They kick food into their mouths with six pairs of feathery legs.

A baby barnacle is swimming and looking for a nice, rocky place to live. Just as it is getting tired, it sees an empty spot on a rock. It makes its own glue and sticks its head to the rock. Here it will grow a shell with little pointed doors that click open and shut.

Barnacles and mussels eat plankton. Plankton are hundreds of different kinds of tiny plants and animals that float in the ocean. There may be 50,000 in a gallon of sea water!

barnacle larva
sticking its head
to rock

magnified plankton

The tide is going out again now, so the octopus heads back to deeper water. Little silver-sided fish seem to be playing hide and seek in the seaweed. The fish have been washed in by the waves and are stuck in the tide pool until the next high tide.

One mummichaug refuses to wait for the tide to come in. It uses its tail to flip itself out of the water, and will walk across the rock on its fins to get back into the ocean.

freckled blenny

naked goby

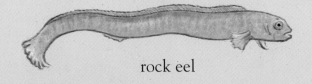

rock eel

We call our planet Earth, but most of it is covered with water. This water is home to animals that are as mysterious as creatures from another planet.

In this world, a crab can regrow a lost leg. How can it do that? Nobody knows. How can a sea slug eat the stinging arms of an anemone without getting stung? Nobody knows. There are more questions than there are answers. Scientists are still trying to solve these mysteries.

The tide pool is like a window into the ocean world. We can see how perfectly nature balances the needs of the plants and animals there. Let's make sure that we don't let pollution spoil it all. There are so many things we get from the edge of the sea. Will the next important medicine come from a tide pool creature? Maybe someday you will be the scientist who answers that question, "Yes!" Maybe YOU will be the one to solve some of the mysteries of the tide pool.

Text and illustrations Copyright © 1992
by Charlesbridge Publishing
Library of Congress Catalog Card Number 92-74498
ISBN 0-88106-483-1 (reinforced for library use)
ISBN 0-88106-482-3 (softcover)
Publishing by Charlesbridge Publishing,
85 Main Street, Watertown, MA 02472
(617) 926-0329 • www.charlesbridge.com
All rights reserved, including the right of
reproduction in whole or in part in any form.
Printed in the United States of America
(hc) 10 9 8 7 6 5 4 3 2 1
(sc) 10 9 8 7 6 5 4 3 2 1